THE CENTURY OF PRINT

BAUHAUSBÜCHER

EDITORS:
WALTER GROPIUS
L. MOHOLY-NAGY

J. J. P. OUD

DUTCH ARCHITECTURE

10

J. J. P. OUD

DUTCH ARCHITECTURE

LARS MÜLLER PUBLISHERS

PRINTING: DZA DRUCKEREI ZU ALTENBURG
REPRODUCTION: INTEGRAL LARS MÜLLER
TYPOGRAPHY, COVER AND JACKET:
L. MOHOLY-NAGY ● BAUHAUS ● DESSAU

Originally published in German under the title of "Holländische Architektur" by Albert Langen Verlag München in 1926, printed by Hesse & Becker Leipzig, printing blocks by Sickert & Reiche Dessau.
First English edition published by Lars Müller, based on the first German edition. Translation by Helen Ferguson.

ISBN 978-3-03778-663-5
Printed in Germany
www.lars-mueller-publishers.com

CONTENTS

CONFESSION

NO ONE EXPECTS ME TO CREATE AN IMMOBILE TABLEAU OF DETACHED HISTORICAL FACTS.

I AM NOT AN ART HISTORIAN BUT AN ARCHITECT: THE FUTURE IS MORE IMPORTANT TO ME THAN THE PAST, AND I AM MORE INCLINED TO INVESTIGATE WHAT IS TO COME THAN TO RESEARCH WHAT HAS ALREADY OCCURRED.

HINDSIGHT HOWEVER OFFERS A SOLID BASIS FOR LOOKING AHEAD: WHAT HAS HAPPENED TEACHES LESSONS FOR WHAT IS TO COME. THE FOLLOWING REFLECTIONS STEM FROM THESE CONSIDERATIONS.

AS A FRIEND TOLD ME, I HAVE BEEN VERY “CRAFTY” ABOUT THIS: PRESENTING MY OWN THOUGHTS UNDER THE GUISE OF AN UNFOLDING FILM ON THE EVOLUTION OF DUTCH ARCHITECTURE. MAYBE HE IS RIGHT: A LEOPARD CAN’T CHANGE ITS SPOTS!

HOWEVER, TO MY MIND, THE LINE OF DEVELOPMENT THAT IS SHOWN APPEARS TO RUN STRAIGHT AND TRUE; SHOULD IT SEEM CROOKED TO OTHERS, I INSIST ON MY RIGHT TO CONSIDER IT TO BE STRAIGHT. FOR THAT LINE IS THE MAIN POINT FOR ME, THE MATERIAL PRESENTED IS SECONDARY.

IF SOMEONE WISHES TO CALL THIS ATTITUDE A PERSONAL ONE, THEY SHOULD FEEL FREE TO DO SO. THE GOAL HOWEVER REMAINS: UNIVERSALITY TAKEN TO ITS LOGICAL EXTREME! UNIVERSALITY ALSO IN AS MUCH AS AN ATTEMPT WAS MADE TO GAIN A CLOSER VIEW OF THE GENERAL ARCHITECTURAL IDEA OF OUR TIME, OVER AND ABOVE DUTCH ARCHITECTURE.

SPEECH OBLIGES US TO TAKE ACTION; THE WORD COMPELS THE DEED!

I HAVE RESPONDED TO THE MORAL GUILT OF MY THEORIZING BY DEPICTING MY OWN WORK; I APOLOGIZE FOR THIS LACK OF MODESTY.

J. J. P. OUD

THE DEVELOPMENT OF MODERN ARCHITECTURE IN HOLLAND

PAST PRESENT FUTURE

As with all other perpetually evolving phenomena, it is difficult to determine where to start and finish when seeking to discuss the modern architecture of Holland. No clear starting point can be determined for — let us call it — modernity and consequently no clear starting point for the lecture.

For that reason, only an excerpt will be shown of what has evolved in our time from developments in the past; subsequently, an attempt shall be made to derive conclusions from this for guidelines that should be followed and further elaborated in future.

There is presently much talk of modernity: too much, some say. I cannot entirely agree with that. The "modern," the contemporary, even as a dimension contingent upon a particular era, has always stirred artists powerfully and triggered their intense engagement in periods of artistic revival. I do not believe that there is some automatism whereby a style can be born — as if self-generated. "Style" always presupposes an intellectual order, i.e. an intellectual volition, even if the intent does not always emerge as clearly as at the dawn of the Renaissance.

Nevertheless, one can concede that nothing is more relative and ephemeral than "modernity," with its external appearance that is, and must always be, different, in keeping with its inherent mutability.

The "modern" can be defined as what is "changing" in the sense of "becoming," i.e., something that is "evolving." Accordingly, the "modern" is not always necessarily simultaneously the "new." The "modern" is that which is coming into being individually, the "new" is that which is coming into being collectively,

**Fig. 1 P. J. H. CUYPERS,
Rijksmuseum in Amsterdam, 1876**

**Fig. 2 P. J. H. CUYPERS,
Amsterdam Central Station, 1880**

2•

a distinction that is of fundamental significance for the development of art; I shall return to its importance in the course of this lecture.

If we define the "modern" and the "new" as that which is coming into being individually and that which is coming into being collectively, this gives rise to the state of affairs mentioned initially, namely that we can never speak of the beginning of the "modern" or the "new." Cause and effect are inextricably linked and perpetually succeed one another as events unfold: there is no beginning and no end: there is only motion.

If we nevertheless attempt to determine a point of departure in this eternal motion, it will only be possible to track it down in epochs in which development has proceeded more by leaps and bounds than continuously; in which the transitional stages of becoming have thus grown more clearly apparent.

Even with this caveat, it is still not possible to demarcate any boundaries: in the interest of a clear account, however, and also as a reflection of this outstanding creative personality, it would be fair to say that the sea-change that produced Dutch modern architecture began when Cuypers arrived on the scene.

Cuypers was the first to disrupt the aesthetic self-gratification underlying the periodic alternation of Romantic and Classicist stylistic imitations that dominated Dutch architecture after the Empire. He once again established a contrast between the objectivity of a deftly deployed yet emotionally deficient form-driven tradition, which is the quintessence of what is known as style-based architecture, and the subjectivity of an elementary artistic sensibility: a subjectivity — as must unfortunately be added immediately — whose unrestrained proliferation could harm Dutch architecture of the future just as much as its seed has fostered today's architecture.

Cuypers, who brought the vital element back into architecture, did not himself progress beyond a subjective interpretation of style-based architecture. From time to time, he also worked with Classicist forms, but, as a true pupil of Viollet-le-Duc, he limited himself, especially in his extensive church-building practice, primarily to utilization of Gothic forms. Besides this preference for Gothic formal language, he also emphasized Gothic rational-structural principles. As a result — apart from his importance for the rebirth of architectural vitality — he also had the merit of providing the impetus for a form of rationalism whose value for Dutch architecture later became apparent, especially in Berlage's oeuvre.

It is clear from what has been said that Cuypers primarily paved the way conceptually for the new architecture of Holland. The vanguard of the subsequent generation of architects focused on elaborating as consistently and purposefully as possible the principles he had evoked, which were still very unclear. On the one hand, they strove for consistent rationalism; on the other hand, they increasingly endeavored to instill into architecture a primal emotional content, which had become a completely alien aspect for academicism (style-based architecture). Both tendencies — inherent opposites, as becomes particularly apparent in their later development — were initially united by the primitive nature of their intentions.

Along with the inner connection between Cuypers's views and the aspirations of the generation that succeeded him, noteworthy links to the formal language of Cuypers's later secular buildings can also be found in the outward appearance of the earliest modern works, especially in Berlage's designs and buildings, which shall be addressed in greater detail. The Rijksmuseum (Fig. **1**) and the Central Station (Fig. **2**) in Amsterdam deserve particular mention.

In positive terms, the influence of Cuypers's secular buildings on the design of these first modern buildings was minimal. The new task at hand was breaking free from their formal language, rather than expanding that language. Nevertheless, positive values for the emerging art most definitely grew out of this process of discarding older formal traditions and its close association with building up new design material. Studying the course of development in detail reveals that the origin of those values can be traced back to Cuypers. A series of preliminary designs by Berlage for the Amsterdam Stock Exchange building is especially instructive in this regard. (Fig. **3, 4, 5, 6**)

It is the tragedy of every concept of art directed toward the elementary, as represented essentially by the entire modern art movement, that it always sets itself the goal of free design that draws on primitive origins, yet that it subsequently, however, repeatedly proves to constitute the consolidation of a more or less violently suppressed design tradition.

Fig. 3 H. P. BERLAGE, First design for the Amsterdam Stock Exchange, 1897

Fig. 4 H. P. BERLAGE, Second design for the Amsterdam Stock Exchange, 1897

Fig. 5 H. P. BERLAGE, Third design for the Amsterdam Stock Exchange, 1897

Fig. 6 H. P. BERLAGE, Amsterdam Stock Exchange, 1898

No phenomenon — not even artistic phenomena — can escape the laws of causality. There are more or less regular and more or less irregular, i.e. evolutionary and revolutionary, transitional forms. Evolution builds up first and destroys afterwards; revolution destroys first and builds up afterwards. Essentially, however, even the latter does not evade causality and can at most escape what has preceded it purely in external terms.

This is unquestionably a shortcoming in our creative faculty, which we must never forget; but, instead of paralyzing us, it should spur us on all the more to perpetual rebellion, to constant revision. The task of art in the throes of renewal is not only the creation of form, but also the destruction of form. Destruction and construction — construction and destruction, that is the alternating current of artistic evolution.

The greater the distance between these two poles, the smaller the absolute value of art, yet the more intensive the activity of development: this is a fact from which — incidentally — the pros and cons of the form-shattering urge emerge in the art of our time, in other words, in Futurism, Cubism, Expressionism, etc., and their apotheosis: Dadaism.

This process of destruction and construction, without which one can never come closer to the primitive nature of artistic creation, essentially only began in Dutch architecture of the last century after Cuypers.

Although in this context the work of artists such as De Bazel, Lauweriks, De Groot, etc., should undoubtedly not be forgotten, the major developmental lineage continues primarily in Berlage, who can therefore be called the precursor of the new Dutch architecture. Although Cuypers disrupted the indifference embodied in constant repetition of historical templates, the great reckoning with style-based architecture emerged in Berlage's oeuvre. Where Cuypers ended, Berlage began.

At the start of his career and before advocating rationalism, Berlage, a pupil of one of Semper's disciples, had deployed conventional forms in every way and examined every conceivable possibility of combining these. He inter alia used Renaissance-style forms for a department store in Kalverstraat in Amsterdam; he worked with Gothic-style forms in elaborating a competition entry for the facade of Milan Cathedral; finally, he used the entire arsenal of Classicist, Gothic-style and Renaissance-style forms in drawing up a powerful design for a mausoleum: an apotheosis of style-based architecture. (Fig. **7**)

The latter design seems to embody the pinnacle of an entire epoch that also constituted its turning point. An apogee of academicist compilation of forms, it also aptly demonstrates the dead end that had been reached in terms of options for architecture to develop.

It was impossible to extend architectural means on this plane by exploitating contentless forms: consolidation was all that remained as an option for further progress.

Cuypers had strived to attain architectural consolidation within the framework of style-based architecture by means of its subjectivation; Berlage, who little by little recognized the shortcomings of this indirect process and gradually grasped the essence of the consequences arising from Cuypers's endeavors, increasingly attempted to push through to the primal ground of development of architectural form. Taking this ground as his starting point, he wished to arrive organically, in other words, moving outwards from the interior, at a direct form of architectural design.

As has already been mentioned, such a reformation is predicated in equal measure upon creative and destructive activity. Clarity of creation can therefore seldom be achieved at once: instead, initially there will be an entangled picture of conflicting efforts, which is not satisfactory from a purely aesthetic point of view. This is also the case in Berlage's earliest modern designs.

The significance of a work of art, however, may only be judged correctly from an absolute vantage point, while the significance of an act can only be judged precisely from a relative vantage point. Even if Berlage's works during this transitional period are more tragic than beautiful in their complicated composition, his approach was at the same time of inestimable value for the future of Dutch architecture, for a perspective of endless possibilities for development was thus opened up to it.

Fig. 7 H. P. BERLAGE, Design for a mausoleum, 1889

In its ultimate leanings, Cuypers's rationalism was also still mainly primarily of a limited aesthetic nature. In its derivation from the Gothic, it could be traced back to Viollet-le-Duc's axiom that all architectural ornament should emerge from the structure, while in the Gothic style greater attention was also paid to architecture's purpose and its logical realization than was the case for architecture under the influence of academicism.

Berlage's rationalism, on the other hand, was actually more in keeping with the concept, which is why it spanned a much wider area. He referred as logically as possible to all vital phenomena that had any direct or indirect connection to architecture; rationalism — one might say — became a rational ethos in his work.

With this breadth of opinion, his approach automatically touched upon the endeavors of largely like-minded pioneers abroad, such as Wagner, Van de Velde, etc. In its intentions, architecture thus once again became an international matter, even if the preliminary results assumed forms that were highly differentiated nationally. In short, its tendencies amounted to achieving an artistic embodiment grounded in the specificity of contemporary life's practical requirements, as well as focusing on the achievements of today's technology, which were fully recognized and appreciated on all fronts. In keeping with this, its purpose was to achieve contemporary architecture with a form also uniformly adapted to modern manifestations of life, so that its harmony with the environment would in the long run give rise to the new style.

A program therefore that is just as topical today as it was then.

Any artist who faces up to the challenge of ideals for the future has only a certain amount of revolutionary activity at his disposal in the sense of a mutation that presses forward to the future. It is not only the past that holds him back, but for the true artist, who is not solely a revolutionary, like all too many in our time, revolution is always a means, never an end in itself. If he has a strong tendentious disposition, initially the urge to address the problem, a love of art, will predominate, and he will drive forward more than creating something moving; gradually the opposition balances itself out, until finally the love of art prevails over the urge to address the problem, and he will create something moving rather than forging ahead. He will then surrender completely to art, cultivate what has been achieved, and strive only incidentally to tackle the problem.

After Berlage, as a pioneer, had given an impetus for radical change whose full import cannot yet be grasped, his oeuvre also struck a balance between the opposing forces of destructive and constructive tendencies and his love of art outshone the urge to solve problems. Since then, in exercising his art, he has created works that number among the very best that Dutch architecture has produced in the distant past or more recently. The restraint of these works stems from his academic training, while breaking away from academicism gave rise to the design freedom manifested in them. (Fig. **8**)

In view of the style problem, however, a great deal of traditional ballast still adheres to Berlage's work. In practice, his broader leaning towards rationalism was still too often limited in practice to the narrower approach of Viollet-le-Duc: technical structural imperatives are still too obtrusive in his design, which is not rooted sufficiently consistently in the practical imperatives of life. It is however precisely with regard to those latter concerns that architecture lags behind the times. Even though structural concerns occupy a noble place in the overall complex of the architectural design process, the structural requirements of any chair, lamp, or house should not be more or less the starting point for its aesthetic design; instead, this should be rooted primarily in the practical needs of comfortable seating, good lighting, comfortable dwelling, a dust-free environment, etc.: these are needs which, especially in our age of refined living options, one can rightly expect will be satisfied as fully as possible.

Technology assumed new design forms, especially in characteristic products such as automobiles, electrical and plumbing-related articles, cutlery, medical instruments, etc., because it devoted its attention to the practical needs of life without any ancillary considerations.

This does not mean that architecture and technology can be equated, as a certain kind of mechanical aesthetics likes to do. One of the reasons why that is simply not possible is that architecture, even in its organic form, must still take into account optical relations arising from the situation, while technology, on the other hand, can, without further ado, design functionally. However, if indications of an elementary, contemporary desire for a collective, that is, new, design are to be found anywhere, it is in technology. Although it admittedly cannot function as a model for architecture in this respect, it can serve as incitement and guidance.

Fig. 8 H. P. BERLAGE, Design for a "Beethovenhuis" in Bloemendaal, 1908

Fig. 9 H. P. BERLAGE, Office building in London, 1914

Although Berlage was still guided too predominantly by structural considerations in his design, he however also pursued this approach too inconsistently to arrive at new architectural forms as a result of this alone. While advocating designs reflecting their specific character for the new structural options, materials, and methods of working, in practice, he primarily used these in combination with and on the basis of conventional building methods, which he adapted to them. As a consequence, he engaged more with their artistic exploitation than with their aesthetic design. Instead of working towards concise, simple and streamlined design that would correspond to the new construction materials' seamlessness, sophistication and mechanical mode of production, he limited himself principally to a more detailed, lively and varied style of design that corresponded to the many joints and imperfections of older building materials and their artisanal mode of production.

It was only in a later office building in London that he sought a solution in practice that was more in keeping with his theoretical views. In this work, he thus arrived at an almost completely different form of design, which simultaneously — as if of its own accord — struck a balance between the occasionally disturbing contrast between the primitive nature of some conventional materials, such as brick, wood, cut stone, etc., and the refinement of new materials, such as plate glass, steel, concrete, majolica, etc. (Fig. **9**)

The points addressed should have made clear that in Dutch architecture, as in architecture generally, a whole field of development concerning the style problem still lies fallow. The rather strange upheaval that occurred in Dutch architecture after the stabilization of Berlage's view can thus more readily be understood in psychological terms rather than explained logically.

His principles and the almost ascetic appearance of his buildings compared with the hollow opulence of works in the academic spirit have made the sobriety of Berlage's art almost proverbial. However, often restraint contains as much passion as does release; it is not the goal that artists set but the manner in which they strive to attain it that determines the nature of a work of art.

Fig. 10 M. DE KLERK, Apartment block for Mr. Hille in Amsterdam, 1911

Accordingly, viewed in their own right, Berlage's works that are rather lively and replete with an inner motion could be called romantic rather than sober, due to the passionate struggle for an organic architecture that gives rise to their design. Nevertheless, Berlage's oeuvre was characterized by pronounced reserved tendencies, not only as a result of this striving for objectivity, but likewise as a consequence of his general and monumental views of architecture, in which individual freedom, scarcely had it cast off its fetters, was immediately subordinated to the laws of a higher concept of beauty.

Generally however, freedom newly acquired is all the keener to savor its liberty before submitting to the yoke once again. While Berlage — by virtue of his masterful self-control — primarily developed rationalism out of the rational and subjective tendencies that emerged from Cuypers, the generation that succeeded him surrendered wholeheartedly to subjectivism, in reaction, in a sense, to this restraint of Berlage.

What is known as the Amsterdam School, whose proponents Kramer and Van der Mey should be mentioned, along with De Klerk as its most talented representative, drags the art of architecture completely into the realm of the romantic and fantastic, without paying the slightest attention to the problem of style.

A sea change of such fundamental importance as this cannot of course be explained solely by a need to react. It is likely that some of the possibilities of newer construction techniques, such as mortar, concrete, brick, tile, new approaches in roofing, etc., which tempt to indulgence in excess, have also contributed. Moreover, the products of architecture became increasingly related to housing construction, with a dwindling focus on monumental buildings, which may have prompted a preference for a solution in the spirit of excess rather than an approach more appropriate to the nature of the task. The latter approach gives rise to only rather inferior artistic results.

Be that as it may, a separate study would be required to do justice to these details. In the context of the overall development, however, what remains very strange is that this upheaval — as demonstrated by an early work by De Klerk: an apartment block for Mr. Hille (Fig. **10**) and, in a certain sense, also the Van der Mey Shipping Office building (Fig. **11**) in Amsterdam — can ultimately be traced back to a much greater degree to style-based architecture than to Berlage. Although Berlage had an undeniable influence on the course of development, it was more indirect than direct. As it flourished, the Amsterdam School proved to be fertilized incidentally by Berlage's architecture rather than emerging from it. (Fig. **12**) In its signature manifestation, it is ultimately characterized by a strangeness and extravagance that departs in every respect from conventional architecture, be it in the academicist or the modern vein. (Fig. **13**)

Rationalism in all its forms has been completely renounced and its opposition to subjectivism — an opposition that can only be bridged on an elevated plane by balancing internal tensions — is evident in all its acuity. The newly conquered principle of organic architecture is once again completely lost. The emphasis of architecture, which had been shifted from the exterior to the interior via Cuypers and Berlage, is now shifted outside once again. Architectural design develops not from the practical needs of the era, the demands of life, but instead external appearance becomes the main dimension of architectural attention from the outset in the creative process, with purpose subsequently adapted to this appearance. Inspiration that evades reality, the architectural vision, prevails entirely: reality becomes a secondary matter, subordinated to the main concern, the facade. The streetscape becomes the foundation of architectural design.

Even if one is completely dismissive of the essence of this architecture, which negates the principles of architecture in every respect, one must admit that at its best, especially in De Klerk's works, it has developed a most peculiar talent.

A dearth of rules pushed to extremes; a plethora of endlessly varied motifs for windows, doors, balconies, oriels, etc.; a boldness in adopting compositions often entirely at odds with structural considerations purely for the sake of form; the use of completely unsuitable materials for the sake of color alone; superbly executed craftsmanship in highly personal detailing; a spirited yet irrational conception of volumes motivated solely by aesthetics; these are some of the elements and characteristics deployed by artists who work along these lines and which their most talented representatives, regardless of all their diversity, manage to hold together so forcefully that their union gives rise to edifices

Fig. 11 J. M. VAN DER MEY, Shipping office building in Amsterdam, 1912

Fig. 12 P. KRAMER, Seamen's home in Den Helder, 1914

Fig. 13 M. DE KLERK,
Design for apartment blocks on the periphery of a small town, 1916

Fig. 14 M. DE KLERK,
Apartment blocks at Spaarndammerplantsoen in Amsterdam, 1913

that take the form of large building envelopes, with coloring, flat surfaces and volumes held in tension, exuding a highly mobile rhythm in the streetscape in a very original and often generous manner, for all their multitude of forms. (Figs. **14–19.**)

Just as this rhythm, in its ruthless drive for self-realization, lacks any underpinning of architectural logic, all this virtuoso architecture reveals itself to be the consequence of an artistic worldview that exists only in and for itself and whose representatives plunge far too deeply into the exquisite possibilities of their own talent to be capable of subordinating these to the objective principles without which it is, ultimately, impossible to achieve either high or general architecture.

While the importance of this architecture in and of itself is thus mainly individual, it also has general significance in the overall evolution of Dutch architecture, which makes its appearance very important, even if viewed from a negative vantage point.

It is namely thanks to these architects that the tendency they advocate, so markedly opposed to Berlage's art, prevented Berlage's design from becoming petrified into a modern tradition in his successors' works. The risk posed by great predecessors is precisely that they become models in form, not in essence. However, realization of contemporary architecture is still in its infancy today: any willingness to accept that any kind of personal design apparatus persists can only lead for now to premature formalism and thus to a new academicism. Formal results must repeatedly be examined anew in their essence, destroyed in their appearance, corrected in the light of the ultimate goal.

Even if not intentionally in this context, the Amsterdam School, in its negation of Berlage's design, had a redemptive effect in the sense that it kept a pathway open that would allow Dutch architecture to develop further. Moreover, its assault on every form of architectural logic provoked such a strong reaction, tipping the scales in the opposite, that is, objective, direction, that it has become associated — as if of its own accord — with the efforts of a newly emerging movement that seems increasingly to be turning its attention to the problem of style.

Fig. 15 M. DE KLERK, Spaarndammerplantsoen apartment blocks in Amsterdam, 1914

Fig. 16 M. DE KLERK, Spaarndammerplantsoen apartment blocks in Amsterdam, 1917

Fig. 17 **M. DE KLERK,
Spaarndammerplantsoen apartment blocks in Amsterdam, 1917**

Fig. 18 M. DE KLERK, Amstellaan apartment blocks in Amsterdam, 1920

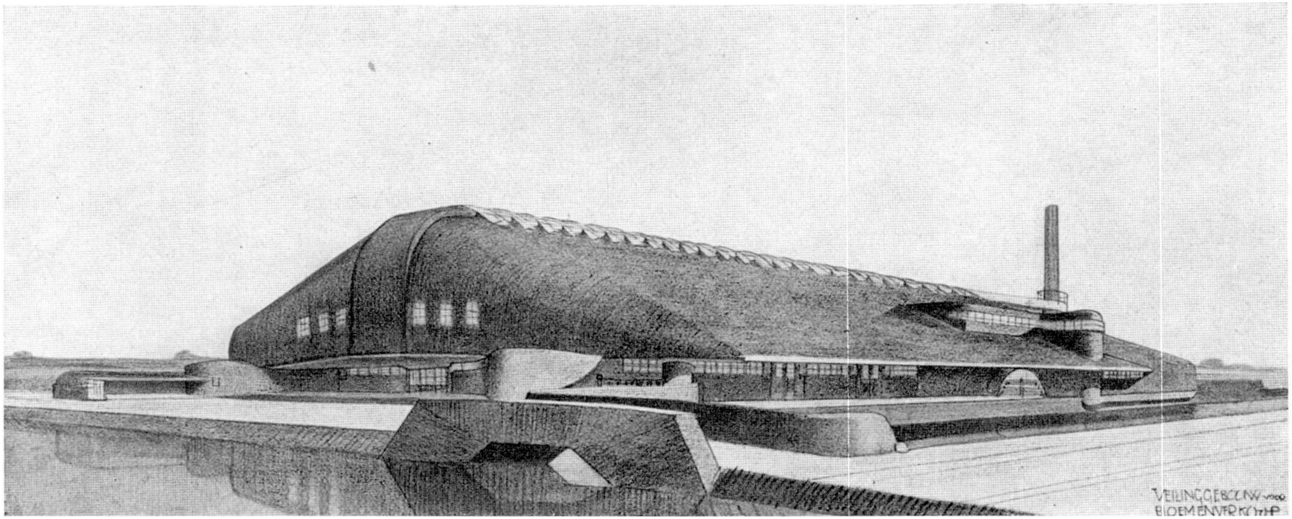

Fig. 19 M. DE KLERK, Design for a flower auction house in Aalsmeer, 1922

This new movement, which is only in its infancy, is for the time being still rather complicated, because two strands are emerging in it, the force of linear and cubic tendencies, outwardly both seemingly merging, while inwardly fundamentally different in nature.

The first strand, which takes the work of the great American architect Wright as its model, admires his work more than it understands his principles. The basis of a new, organic architecture, however — as must be emphasized again and again — can never be constituted by an external form, but should always be constituted by an inner necessity. Any interpretation into it of old or new traditions of form degrades the art of architecture from an experience to a matter of taste, i.e. from aesthetic design to a style-based architecture.

In this respect, the intensive development of the liberal arts of today, whose offshoots more or less merge with the second strand of the new architectural movement in Holland, is particularly instructive. (Figs. **20–29**) In striving for independent aesthetic-organic design, as it emerges from the "isms" of the present, the fine arts increasingly do not produce from the exterior moving inwards, but rather from the interior moving outwards, less and less as a representation, more and more as a formation. Even if it is not possible when merging with such a purely aesthetic movement to exclude any risk that some kind of artistic externalities dictated from above might be interpreted into architecture, this is counterbalanced by the fact that even architectural design that develops purely organically from function must correspond to some kind of formal aesthetic intention. However, the significance of the new art movement is precisely that it represents more of an urge-for-form than a being-form: in accordance with its principles, it corrects itself again and again anew in line with the manifestation of form, in order to liberate itself with ever greater consistency from any addition that is inorganic, that is, merely external.

The practical and aesthetic, material and spiritual inclinations of the time are to be found in this striving to eliminate all inorganic means and attain solely organic means, in this drive, therefore to move from the trivial to the objective. The power of the means deployed, which is becoming increasingly apparent as a consequence of collective tendencies, thus forms the precept that informs the new style.

Fig. 20 J. J. P. OUD, Design for a row of houses by the sea, 1917

Fig. 21 J. J. P. OUD, Design for a factory building in Purmerend, 1919

Fig. 22 J. B. VAN LOGHEM, Hall, "Rosehaghe" residential ensemble in Haarlem, 1920

Fig. 23 J. B. VAN LOGHEM, “Rosehaghe” residential ensemble in Haarlem, 1920

Fig. 24 W. M. DUDOK, School building in Hilversum, 1921

Fig. 25 G. RIETVELD, Kalverstraat jewelry store in Amsterdam, 1922

Fig. 26 G. RIETVELD, Interior of Kalverstraat jewelry store in Amsterdam, 1922

Fig. 27 G. RIETVELD, Consulting room of a doctor in Maarssen, 1922

Fig. 28 **G. RIETVELD, Private house in Utrecht, 1924**

Fig. 29 **G. RIETVELD, Interior (Private house in Utrecht), 1924**

In architectural terms, this relates first and foremost — to explain this in passing — to removing ornamentation. (Figs. **30–36**)

The ornament is to architecture, one might say by way of comparison, what an object from the world of nature is to painting, i.e. an unsuitable means and a secondary matter. Ornament on a building is — like an object from the world of nature in a painted canvas — not simply an organ of the overall organism, the work of art, but also at the same time an organism in its own right. In addition to its eccentric, i.e. spatial, relations to the work as a whole — which are, at best, of a symbolic-structural nature, as in the Middle Ages — it also has concentric, i.e. restrictive, relations to its own being that exist only in extrinsic connection to the whole. An aesthetic duality therefore emerges from the overall impression, disrupting not only the uniform, organic nature of the whole but also hampering an architectural synthesis that is sought in every respect in keeping with the zeitgeist.

Although no design method seems more intricately entangled than in architecture, given its diverse and heterogeneous components, the requisite factors can in fact ultimately be divided into two more or less strictly separated groups. On the one hand, there are practical factors relating to purpose, material, working method and structural design; on the other hand, there are the nonmaterial factors of artistic emotion that must combine the various, often contradictory elements into an aesthetic and practical unity. Even if practical factors — and above all the purpose — form the underpinning for architectural design, ultimately an equilibrium between these two groups is always attained by harmonious design, with each making sacrifices to accommodate the other.

However, our time, in its mental deadening, knows only the charm of pronounced one-sidedness. Because the practical factors of architecture — with the exception of its purpose — are all subject to the progress of our technical development, with, moreover, as already mentioned, remarkable points of contact between technology and architecture, in the modern movement there were initially architects who were purely technicians and who, in their one-sided admiration for technology, entirely neglected the aesthetic side of the problem. Alarmed by the disappointments of their own — thus inevitable — failure, they subsequently became the pure romantics of our day, entirely

Fig. 30 P. J. C. KLAARHAMER, Design for apartment blocks in Utrecht, 1919

7 •

Fig. 31 **J. J. P. OUD, “Spangen” apartment blocks in Rotterdam, Pieter Langendijkstraat, 1919**

Fig. 32 J. J. P. OUD, "Tusschendijken" apartment blocks in Rotterdam, Gysingstraat, 1920

Fig. 33 J. J. P. OUD, “Tusschendijken” apartment blocks in Rotterdam, Taandersstraat, 1920

Fig. 34 J. J. P. OUD, Courtyard of "Tusschendijken" apartment blocks in Rotterdam, 1920

Fig. 35 L. C. VAN DER VLUGT,
Vocational college in Groningen, 1922

negating technology with their one⸗sided love of aesthetics, and consequently failing once again.

The goal of architectural creativity should be not only technology but also aesthetics, not only intellect and not only emotion, but rather the harmonious unification of both. A fundamental consideration in this process remains that reality above all forms the point of departure for aesthetic design. Predetermination of any kind of formal scheme that does not correspond to this reality — and now I am also thinking of the aforementioned cubic design, in which Dutch architecture once again runs the risk of ossifying in a new design dogma instead of continuing to work on its inner (purifying) tendencies — every presupposition, therefore, of a one⸗sided aesthetic conception of form that does not correspond to function is reprehensible, for it violently suppresses the unavoidable necessities of existence and augments the discrepancy between inner and outer life. This dichotomy cannot be overcome by negating reality but only by affirming it. It is a cheerless age that cannot also derive intellectual benefit from material progress!

The technical development of our time has never unfolded its wonders in art. Yet it boasts so many wonders that reality surpasses fantasy!

Machinery affords us scope for streamlined and precise forms that would previously have been inconceivable. In chemistry, we now have undreamt⸗of means and processes for enameling and glazing; options for constructing spans and overcoming gravity in iron⸗based structures; for bending and spreading in glass technology; for joint⸗free structures and cantilevering when building with concrete. These are just a few of the existing possibilities and they all await utilization, which is thwarted again and again by the sentimentality of an outdated, utterly self⸗satisfied view of art.

●

As mentioned above, the second strand of the new Dutch architectural movement increasingly seeks to reappraise the problem of style and the architectural possibilities alluded to here. Incidentally, the urge to do so has now again become international and there does indeed seem once again for the first time to be a solid foundation for achieving general beauty, a style, by attaining an organic architecture, with a simple, clear and streamlined design that is

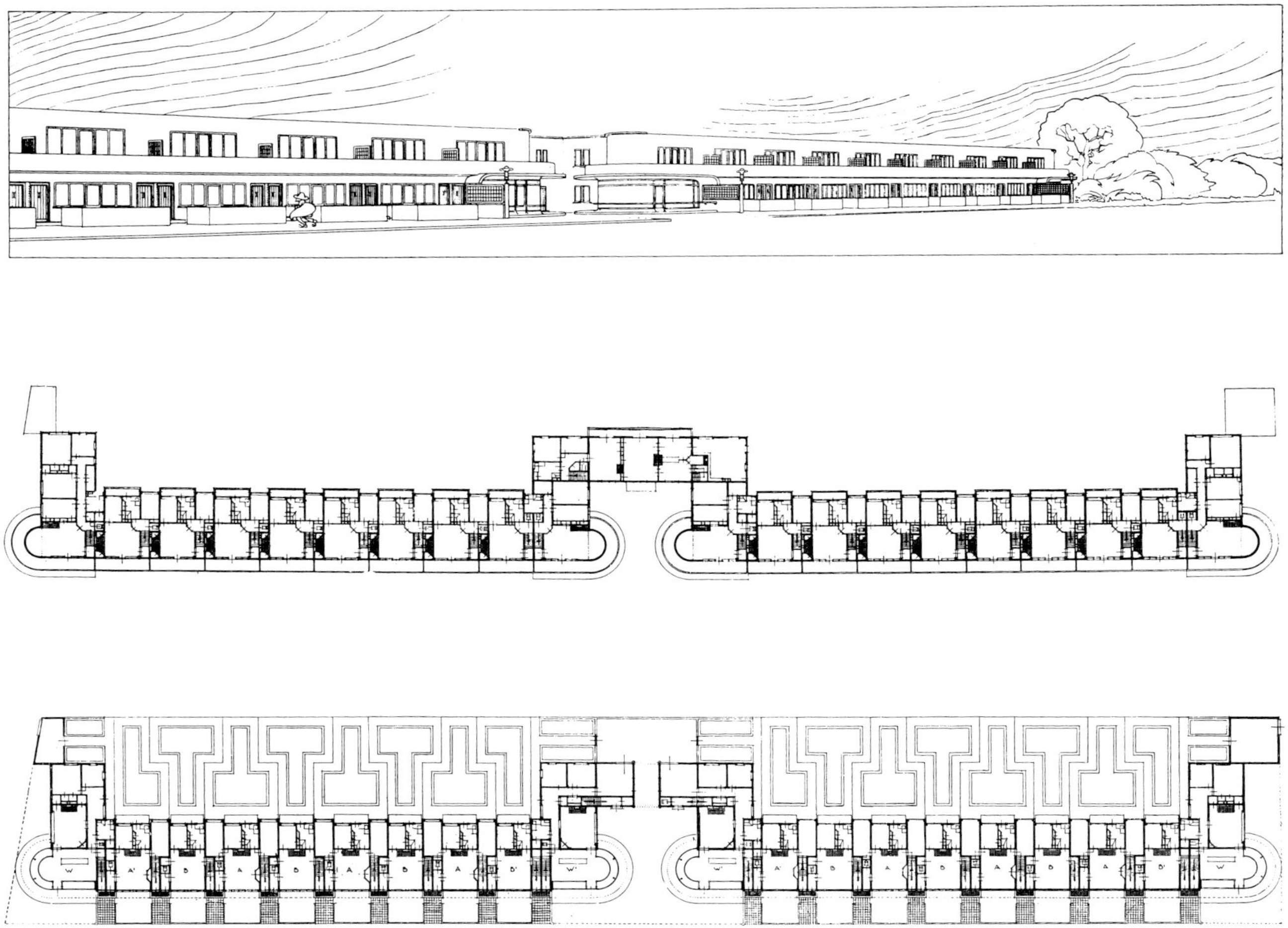

Fig. 36 J. J. P. OUD,
Design for workers' housing in Hoek van Holland (by the sea), 1924

Fig. 37 LE CORBUSIER-SAUGNIER,
Country house in Vaucresson, 1923

Fig. 38 W. GROPIUS with A. MEYER,
Theater in Jena, 1922

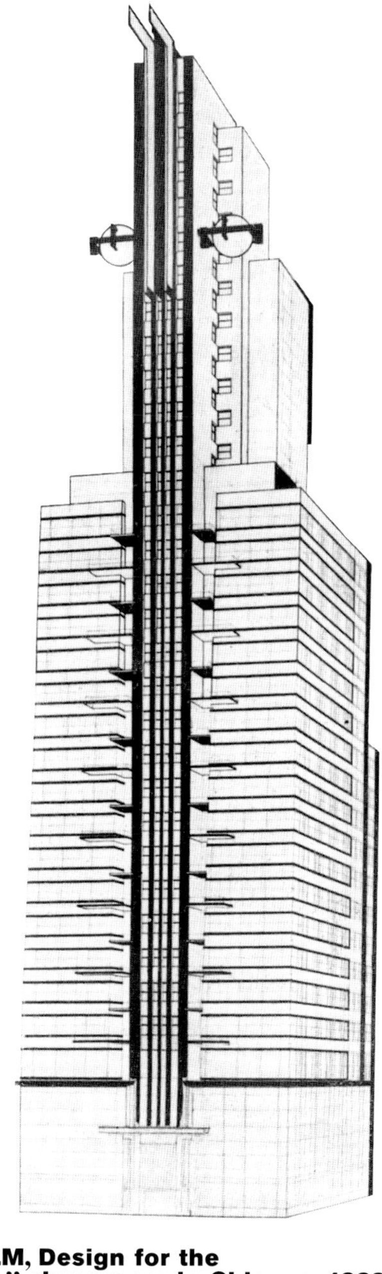

Fig. 39 K. LÖNBERG-HOLM, Design for the "Chicago Tribune" skyscraper in Chicago, 1922

embodied in a dearth of ornamentation and that reflects advances made in technology and lifestyles. (Figs. **37–39**)

This lecture has attempted to indicate where there are points of contact with this major developmental lineage in the evolution of Dutch architecture. This appraisal has revealed that a balance always tends to be struck between the opposing forces of destructive and constructive tendencies, and, as a result, the collective becoming that seeks the new and distant overall beauty is transformed into an individual becoming that generates the modern, the individual work of art. The urge to concentrate on style vanishes again and again into love of art.

From the latter's point of view, contemporary Dutch architecture — as can be asserted with no chauvinism — has achieved something significant, both in the evolution described above and in the works of a few more isolated artists, who have too little to do with overarching developments to merit detailed discussion within a general analysis. Art, however — as should have been demonstrated by the above discussion — is the enemy of style. And although, philosophically speaking, one can claim that a style is not an end point but only a pinnacle and thus at the same time a turning point within a development, it is ultimately these pinnacles which, as the outcome of a strong overall artistic will, have most successfully satisfied the human need for beauty throughout history.

Turning point 1922–1923

ON FUTURE ARCHITECTURE AND ITS ARCHITECTURAL POSSIBILITIES

WRITTEN IN 1921. ALTHOUGH TODAY (1926) THE FACTS ARE ALREADY SOMEWHAT DIFFERENT (AND HAVE ALREADY IMPROVED!), IT SEEMED UNDESIRABLE TO CHANGE THE TEXT. THAT HOLDS TRUE IN PARTICULAR AS NO CORRECTION IS REQUIRED CONCERNING THE TENDENCIES IDENTIFIED, WHICH ULTIMATELY ARE ALL THAT IS BEING ADDRESSED.

Architecture is in an extremely important period for its development, although its importance is not sufficiently recognized in terms of the direction in which that development lies.

After academicism was vanquished, a renewal of architecture has broken fresh ground, although only the initial traces of that renewal's ultimate propensities have become visible.

It is erroneous to conclude — as a consequence of the outdated Ruskinian view that the supreme aesthetic revelation lies in struggle — that this renewal should simultaneously be a climax and therefore also an end.

Life is struggle, but art in its supreme form is about overcoming, i.e., satisfaction. The intellectual, social and technical progress our time can demonstrate has never been realized in architecture to date. It is not merely that contemporary architecture is not ahead of its time; it is not even keeping pace with it, and at times constrains the necessary development of life. This is demonstrated by traffic, health care, and to an extent also housing shortages, to name but a few concerns. Architecture no longer aims to embody the most desirable form of accommodation in a beautiful form, but sacrifices everything and everyone to a predetermined view of beauty that has arisen in other circumstances, becoming an obstacle to full development of our lives. Cause is mistaken for effect and vice versa. This is why all the products of technical progress are not gratefully put to immediate practical use in the building industry, for such products are first examined from the vantage point of the prevailing conception of art and, generally, standing in contradiction to it, struggle to hold their own against the reverential architectural profession.

Plate glass, reinforced concrete, iron, machine⸗manufactured structural and decorative blocks, etc. — to a greater or lesser degree — provide the evidence for this.

●

No art is more difficult to reform than the art of architecture, because in no other art is design more stringently determined by matter. Consequently, no other art has retained more of its external design tradition for centuries than this art of architecture.

It does not recognize destruction for the sake of improved reconstruction: it constantly develops, never regresses. Destruction of external form — so necessary because of constant changes in the circumstances that determine form — did not occur in architecture. The Renaissance drew on the Gothic age, Gothic on Romanesque, Romanesque on Byzantine, etc., and the elements that constitute the actual essence of architecture, the balanced interplay of the forces of load⸗bearing and load, of tensile stress and compressive stress, of action and reaction, were never represented in pure form over the course of time, but always veiled, enveloped in some fantastic disguise.

●

It seems axiomatic that architecture is only consolidated and valued if it is the result of endless further training or abstraction of traditional forms, if all previ⸗ous attempts to animate matter emerge from it in compressed and refined form.

The true value of tradition, however, lies only in art as an expression of interiority, of an attitude to life. A clear concept of tradition, therefore, means rebellion, not submission, vis⸗à⸗vis earlier art.

An era's attitude towards life is the lodestone for its art, not design tradition!

●

Never has that attitude towards life been more introspective than it is now, never has there been a more acute contrast between its contradictions, which are pushed to extremes. Never has there been greater chaos. Natural values are repressed but still exert a pull of attraction; intellectual values emerge but are found repellent. The inevitable consequence of life nevertheless unfolds with resolute exigency: intellect overcomes nature.

Mechanics displaces animal power, philosophy displaces faith. The stability of the old way of life is undermined, the natural connection between its organs is disrupted. New, intellectual life complexes take shape, break away from their old, natural counterparts and seek reciprocal balance. The new attitude towards life begins to disclose itself in an initially unbalanced form. A new rhythm of life is in the making, in which the broad outlines of a new aesthetic energy and a new ideal of form are emerging.

Only architecture, which has the task of reflecting the culture of its time, remains intellectually immune to these developments!

●

The new attitude to life is put into practice for the first time in painting and sculpture in the conscious-aesthetic sense — in the only conceivable, i.e. revolutionary, way for such changed circumstances. Because life has not yet established an equilibrium, this new conception of art rooted in the reality of life has not yet overcome the struggle (the tragedy) either. Here, however, the struggle is a means, not an end, a means to attain the intellectual, the liberating, the purely aesthetic.

In Futurism, with its attempt to reconcile space and time in the art of painting, as well as in Cubism, with its struggle between reality and abstraction, the new attitude towards life is already reflected in the paintings without yet establishing a rhythmic equilibrium. While Futurism can assert itself as the prototype of a new, dynamic art of painting, expressed through the union of cinematography and painting on canvas, Cubism contains more general developmental possibilities, which could distinguish it as a transitional stage in moving toward a new, monumental art of painting.

Cubism outwardly still reveals the tragic image of the transitional period, tossed back and forth as it is between an abstract-structural design urge and a more profound philosophical love of nature, the latter signifying life as it is, i.e.

being and appearance simultaneously, loved and revered in all its forms, yet at the same time rejected in the relativity of its external manifestations.

The transition from the natural to the intellectual, i.e. from representation to formation, or from the limited to the spatial, takes place in Cubism, initially still in a predominantly natural fashion, although revolutionary in essence, and subsequently by dissecting natural form.

Following its inner driving force, its intellectual tendency increasingly supplants the arbitrariness of the natural model; discarding the incidental, streamlining forms and rendering color expansively planar, the consistency of a pure art of painting is asserted and becomes a way to shape space, deploying only painterly means, through balanced positioning and proportioning of colors, and in this form, discarding its existential justification as a painting on canvas, proves to be of the utmost importance in developing color as an element in the architecture of the future.

Architecture itself, the most culturally significant of all the arts, initially moves past this fermentation process, remaining internally unaffected. Intellectually still not tinged by the revolutionary sentiment that gave rise to Cubism, yet not having moved beyond that, it decays outwardly as it passes from one excess to the next, without being able to overcome its natural propensity for the incidental, for ornamentation, in favor of a more intellectual conception that would directly shape the essence of the art of architecture, the taut balance of forces.

What it cannot do, however, by its own intellectual force, comes into being spontaneously through the power of circumstances.

Unlike the fine arts, architecture is not the exclusive result of an intellectual process, but also stems from material factors: from purpose, material and structural considerations. Its goal is twofold: to be simultaneously useful and beautiful. As intellectual factors change over the course of time, material factors also change perpetually, and their development can only temporarily be constrained. This applies to architectural objects just as it does to industrial objects.

However, as the aesthetic possibilities of an object diminish and its utility value increases, resistance to its pure determination of form on the part of the prevailing view of art dwindles.

That makes it possible for objects that mainly have a practical purpose and have aesthetic value only to a limited degree to escape artistic attention, allowing them to be designed to be as fit for purpose as possible, from a purely technical perspective. It then becomes apparent that the human urge for beauty is so pronounced that these objects, as if of their own accord, transcend the purely technical to attain an elementary aesthetic form.

Objects of this kind, such as for example automobiles, steamships, yachts, menswear, sportswear, electrical and sanitary articles, cutlery, etc., as pure expressions of their time, thus in the first instance contain the elements of the new aesthetic design within them and can be regarded as points of contact with outward manifestations of the new art. Through their lack of ornamentation, their streamlined form and flat expanses of color, through the relative perfection of their material and their pure proportions — to a significant extent as a consequence of the new (mechanical) mode of production — these indirectly serve to fertilize architecture in its present form, allowing an urge for abstraction to arise within it — prompted too by more direct causes — that initially reveals itself as the sublimation of conventional forms, not as the manifestation of a new attitude to life.

Over and above the indeterminacy of form, it is above all the lack of aesthetic energy, of intellectual tension that reveals that this urge for abstraction remains negative, i.e. it is the result of life flowing away rather than of its unfurling.

Contemporary architecture — even in its most highly developed form — does not display an awareness of tension that is aesthetically realized in the grand rhythm, the balanced complex of interrelated parts that exert a mutual influence, each supporting the other's aesthetic intention, within which nothing can be added nor removed, with each part so much in proportion to the other parts, in itself and as a whole, that any change — even the smallest alteration — will completely disrupt the equilibrium.

The architecture of today mitigates all of its failure to attain such an equilibrium with its own means by applying ornamentation.

By utilizing ornament, any shortcoming in pure architectural, compositional balance, any architectonically flawed attempt at architectural design can be salvaged extrinsically by architectonic means alone, such as windows, doors, chimneys, balconies, oriels, paint, etc. Ornament is the universal remedy for architectural impotence!

Ornament-free architecture requires the utmost possible purity of architectural composition.

A propensity for unornamented architecture, in as much as it can be derived indirectly from the factors mentioned, as well as directly from factors to be specified in greater detail, has already been repeatedly demonstrated, but has also repeatedly been rejected, since the opinion prevails that the concepts of beauty and decoration are mutually exclusive at the highest level, and because there is a belief in an ingrained human need for decoration. A need that — if it does exist — does not necessarily require satisfaction through art. All ornamentation in art is incidental: external compensation for an internal deficit: an appendage not an organ; only necessary in architecture as long as design fails from an aesthetic point of view when using its own means.

In relation to the whole architectural organism, ornamentation means: external harmony, not internal energy: always only connection — superficial as in the Renaissance or intimate as in the Gothic — but never contrast, never tension.

The history of architecture's development teaches us that the manner of its genesis in the first instance simultaneously contains the seeds of its downfall. The first hut was only decorated once it had been built, thus laying the foundation for the nonsimultaneity that would occur throughout the centuries, and consequently the hermaphroditic fashion in which utility and beauty are shaped, giving rise to the confusing congruence of beauty and decoration that has impeded the emergence of pure architecture and still does so to this day.

Only now does it seem possible, compelled by circumstances and through the expansion of aesthetic insight, to create architecture that shapes itself out of and through its own being, architecture in which the other arts, instead of being applied, i.e. subordinated, cooperate organically, architecture that from the outset experiences beauty through its structural functioning, in other words, elevating the structure itself beyond its material necessity to an aesthetic form as a result of the tense balance of its proportions.

Such architecture does not tolerate ornamentation, because it is per se a complete, space-shaping organism, in which any ornamentation would be individualization and thus a restriction of the universal, i.e. of the spatial.

●

Due to its complexity, the course adopted by architectural evolution cannot be explained in the light of just a few factors. It involves an entire complex of forces that human consciousness is more or less aware of, from which individual, more obvious forces only now and then emerge more clearly and can be demonstrated. When it comes to factors more directly related to architecture itself, changed production methods and new materials in particular have helped pave the way for the revolution in its design.

●

Replacing craftsmanship by machine-driven manufacturing, which is a social and economic necessity, is also beginning to assume ever greater proportions in the construction industry. Initially obstinately held at arm's length by aesthetes, use of mechanically manufactured products is increasingly spreading, despite all resistance, from subordinate auxiliary materials to extremely important components, and influencing designs.

For the time being, this is only expressed in details; however, it is precisely the details — which in this context are only to be understood as ornamental and figural details, decoration — that are the quintessence of the prevailing view of the art of architecture. While still relatively objective in Classicist style-based architecture, now that architecture has overcome academicism, they are growing increasingly unconstrained under the influence of resurgent medieval tendencies.•)

What the bow is to the violinist, the detail is to the contemporary architect: a means of expression par excellence to convey inner movement. The more subjective the artist, the more expressive the detail. The greatest possibilities therefore lie in craftsmanship. The golden age of craftsmanship, the Middle Ages, was therefore also the golden age of detail. The demise of craftsmanship thus also signifies the demise of the detail.

In contrast to the handcrafted detail, i.e. a detail produced used artisanal methods, which — relatively indeterminate in form and color — allows for endless variations on a main motif, the hallmark of the machine-made detail is that, while relatively determined in form and color, it looks completely the same as any other — simultaneously produced — detail of the same type.

It thus inherently lacks the extensive expressive possibilities that the handcrafted detail intrinsically possesses, giving rise to a need to shift the principal focus of architecture's individual emphasis away from the detail per se to concentrate instead on its status and extent within the whole, i.e. to its position in relation to the other components. The personal aspect in the architecture of the future will be shaped not so much in terms of subdivisions and more in the light of mutual relations within the structure of these subdivisions, i.e. in the architectural organism itself.

The significance of the subdivisions as decoration is thus eliminated and is stripped back to the significance of proportion, i.e. form and color within the overall impression.

•) This applies mainly to Holland. Tendencies differ in other countries but the results are similar.

Alongside altered production methods, it is in particular iron, plate glass and reinforced concrete that will have a revolutionary influence on existing architectural design. Designs derived from traditional design do not exist for any of these materials. On the contrary, here too, traditional design was an obstacle to the full blossoming of their possibilities. After great expectations were initially nurtured that iron could lead to a new form of architecture, its erroneous utilization soon pushed it into the background in aesthetic terms.

It has been held to be destined for shaping volumes and surfaces due to its materiality, which is so visible — in contrast, for example, to plate glass, which is only haptically material — yet without any consideration of the way in which the hallmark of an iron construction lies precisely in its scope to withstand maximum forces with minimum quantities of material, as expressed in its supreme form in framework. In its most fitting mode of utilization, iron's typical appearance can also be transparent, more open than closed. Its architectural value consequently lies in shaping emptiness, rather than abundance, i.e. in creating a contrast to the closed nature of the wall surface rather than a continuous extension of that surface.

This is even more obvious for plate glass. Its use eliminated the logical need to divide openings for windows and doors into relatively small segments by means of the familiar mesh of wooden muntins, which in a sense optically extend the closed wall surface across and beyond the opening.

A sheet of plate glass, used unadorned, creates an impression in architecture of being an opening per se. Where the dimensions required make subdivision essential, the sections become so large that only iron muntins ensure sufficient stability; their open character is thus maintained in this context too.

Such a pane of glass is only satisfying as an architectural solution from a structural and aesthetic point of view if it is actually designed as an opening, i.e. if it gives the viewer a sense that it is organically integrated into the architectural ensemble by means of an effective load-distribution system that ensures adequate structural support.

Using only iron and plate glass on this basis will afford scope to boost architecture's openness to such an extent that future architecture will largely be able to overcome its heavy external appearance entirely rationally.

●

Unadulterated use of reinforced concrete opens up similar prospects.

Its aesthetic possibilities are so great — compared to the restrictions that brick imposes on architectural design — that its more extensive use can, in the long term, help salvage design freedom in architecture.

The requisite subordination to certain proportions, the dependency on arch shapes that are likewise determined by these proportions, to a large degree imposes shackles upon designs that use brick.

In addition, as the material is not suited to absorbing tensile stresses — apart from structural engineering exceptions, such as stones suspended on iron wire, etc. — it hampers the construction of reasonably large horizontal spans and cantilevers. Combining the auxiliary materials that thus become necessary: wood, iron, reinforced concrete, etc. with brick produces too heterogeneous a mix to lead to generally satisfactory solutions. Unless plastering is added, it is not possible with brick to create a streamlined, clean line or a pure homogeneous surface; the small parts and large number of joints prevent that.

On the other hand, with reinforced concrete, a homogeneous combination of load-bearing and supported components is possible, as well as significant horizontal extension and clear-cut delimitation of surfaces and volumes. Moreover, in contrast to the old system of load-bearing and supported elements, in which it is only possible to build from the bottom to the top by moving backwards (i.e. towards the rear), it is also possible to build up from the bottom to the top (i.e. moving forwards). This latter option opens up scope for a new plasticity in architecture, which, in combination with the design possibilities of iron and plate glass — deployed structurally — can trigger the emergence of an architecture with a visually immaterial, almost floating appearance.

●

In conclusion, color should also be mentioned as the final important direct factor for architectural renewal.

In today's architecture, the color element generally suffers from pitiful indifference.

On the one hand, this can be explained by the one-sided concentration of painterly interest on the individual case, on the image in fine or applied art and on decoration, but on the other hand, the materials commonly used in architecture today per se constitute so many obstacles to the development of color that no improvement can be expected unless the material is altered. The material used in the composition of walls is especially important in this respect.

In almost every building today, the material used in the walls predominates in terms of volume and therefore its color predominates too. In setting an artistic emphasis in a building — with a balanced color scheme — the choice of the material for the walls is therefore immediately decisive. If the painterly emphasis of the wall material is on the pictural, i.e. on nuance, on mood, the color design of the entire building will thus be dependent on nuance, that is, on mood.

In our country (in Holland) with its predominantly brick construction, the latter is almost always the case. Brick's painterly value — like that of most materials produced by artisanal techniques — is not in its color per se, which overall could be described as brown-gray on the whole, but in the tonalities of its coloring, in nuance. Pure, luminous color has no effect against such backgrounds. It either stands out or is suppressed by the predominant grayness.

Moreover, however, the color value of the brick is natural, in contrast, for example, to that of paint, i.e. its value as such increases as a function of meteorological influences. Since the color value of paint is constant — or at least should be — the chromatic harmony established between brick and paint is liable to change, so that initial harmony can be transformed into discord after a few weeks. A discord that is all the more noticeable when using a light color rather than a more neutral one, which is probably why a preference for stone gray and dark green has so long been standard, especially in the countryside.

In addition to the reasons mentioned earlier, this is also an enduring obstacle to color development when using brick.

Facing and glazed stone, as well as plastered masonry, are already in a more favorable position in this respect.

However, increasingly frequent inventions concerning smooth and light-colored finishes for plaster and concrete surfaces in particular open up such significant prospects for the development of color in architecture that, in combination with the new design possibilities described above, they could completely change the overall aspect of architecture.

●

In summary, one can conclude that architecture rationally based on contemporary living conditions will in every respect stand in contrast to the architecture of the past. Without lapsing into arid rationalism, it will above all be objective, yet in this objectivity it will immediately experience something more sublime. In the acutest possible contrast to the nontechnical, formless and colorless products of current inspiration with which we are familiar, it will shape the tasks set for it with complete devotion to the goal in an almost impersonal fashion, forging these through technology into organisms of clear form and pure proportion. Instead of the natural appeal of uncultivated material, uneven face of the glass, agitated motion within the surface, fading paint, melted glazes, weathered masonry, etc., this architecture will display the allure of cultivated material, the clarity of the glass, sparkling, smoothly rounded surfaces, gleaming and luminous paint, glittering steel, etc.

The tendency within architectonic development thus points to an architecture that in its essence will be more closely tied to the material realm than in the past, while in its manifestations it will move beyond that realm to a greater degree; an architecture that, free of all impressionistic mood-setting, will develop in an abundance of light to encompass pure proportions, luminous colors and organic clarity of form that will surpass classical purity thanks to the absence of anything incidental.

1921

FRANK LLOYD WRIGHT'S INFLUENCE ON EUROPE'S ARCHITECTURE

Although I am convinced of the inadequacy of all value judgments in art when these concern contemporaries or people very close to us, Frank Lloyd Wright towers so high above his surroundings that I can with conviction call him one of the greatest figures of our time without fearing that a later generation will be obliged to reject this judgment.

His oeuvre formed such a well-rounded whole amidst architectural products that in their dearth of style will have to be called the style of the 19th century, such a unity of conception prevailed in the broad overview and in the detail, his creative output was so assertive in its expression and well-defined in the thrust of its development that it remains virtually unparalleled.

If it is intrinsic to this era that even the work of the best still gives you a sense of how it became what it is, in Wright's oeuvre everything exists without conveying any sense of intellectual strain associated with its production. If one admires others for their talent, the way in which one sees them mastering the material, I venerate Wright because the process whereby his work is created remains entirely alien, a complete mystery to me.

It does not at all diminish this veneration, tried-and-tested to a high degree in the shifting phases of one's own development, to state that I find myself simply unable to describe Wright's important, even major, influence on Europe's architecture as felicitous.

This influence unfolded along similar lines to the emergence of a "Wright School" in the American West. Wright himself once wrote of it in a pessimistic moment that he was annoyed to see that the form in which he had realized his concept in his buildings seemed to exert a greater attraction than the concept itself. Since this concept aimed to take function as a starting point rather than form, he held this to have a malign influence on the development of architecture in general.

I would also like to describe as malign in this sense the hypnotic force that Wright's strange talent exerted on architecture on this side of the ocean. In the confused flurry of opinions over the last decades in European architecture, which — after the excessive unity and certainty of earlier generations — instantly turned anything that was not entirely crazy into a nerve-racking problem, it was probably inevitable that Wright's work would seem to be a revelation when it became more thoroughly known. Free of the fussy details that undermined the architecture of the Old World, self-evident despite exotic peculiarities, captivating despite the simplicity of the motifs, Wright's work was immediately convincing.

The stacked volumes, which seemed to have fused with the ground, were so solidly constructed, despite all their mobility, the intermeshing and interpenetrating elements, seeming to flit past as if in a film projected onto a screen, were so natural, the trajectory through the rooms, configured in a sequence with a playful lightness of touch, was so full of integrity that not a shadow of a doubt arose as to the imperative necessity of this formal language for us too, so that we accepted without further ado that here practicality and comfort were combined into a beautiful synthesis in the only way possible for our time; that Wright the artist had accomplished what Wright the prophet proclaimed; that now the long-sought-after ideal had been found, within which universal striving coincided entirely with individual attainment; in a nutshell, that in this case the personal first and foremost finally became universal again. In addition — and certainly no one remained indifferent to this — the use of Wright's means, even where employed with less clarity and less of a virtuoso touch than by the master himself, generally seemed to guarantee a tolerable and stimulating effect.

As a result, the avant-garde of architecture and all those happy to number themselves among its ranks, when everything is going rather smoothly, in Holland, Germany, Czechoslovakia, France, Belgium, Poland, Romania, etc. succumbed with the utmost willingness to the influence of this admirable talent.

The displaced planes, the pronounced projecting panels and cornices, the repeatedly interrupted and subsequently continued volumes, the dominating horizontal thrust of development, all these typical traits of Wright's oeuvre are apparent in the period when the spirit of Wright's creations arrived in our part of the world, as the hallmark of a significant percentage of modern architectural production in Europe.

It is, however, a mistake, which has been made many times by critics and which cannot be pointed out too vigorously (for this misinterpretation is precisely the reason why Wright's influence on Europe's architecture must be described as less than favorable), to attribute the emergence of these characteristics exclusively to Wright. At the time when deification of Wright's works was at its height among his colleagues on this side of the ocean, European architecture was itself seething with energy and Cubism was born!

Just as much as Wright's influence, Cubism must be viewed as playing an important role in the emergence of the characteristic outward forms expressed in the aforementioned strand within European architecture. This strand — one can thus conclude — results itself from a mingling of two influences that in any event is disappointing because for the umpteenth time it points to a cult of form on both sides rather than being guided by the essence; above all however it is disappointing because it led to a loss of vigor in a tendency (the Cubist one), whose consequences promise to be of the greatest importance for the future of architecture. A tendency — moreover — that ultimately would be closer to Wright than paying tribute to exteriority, the unintended side effect generated by others who believed they were glorifying him by imitating his works.

If one sets Cubism's endeavors as a complementary element alongside Wright's influence when considering the factors that fostered the emergence of the aforementioned phenomena, the fascination exerted by Wright's works undeniably paved the way for Cubism to a large extent: an ironic twist of fate subsequently ensured that the compelling lyricism inherent in this architectural Pied Piper's tunes would simultaneously tarnish the purity of the sound beginning to resonate in European architecture, as a result of intentions that should also be Wright's, even if his work sometimes bore witness to those in a somewhat different vein than his volition (his volition as expressed in his writing).

What Wright wanted, namely: an architecture based on the needs and possibilities of its own time, whose demands — general, economic feasibility, universal social accessibility, general social-aesthetic necessity — result in: restraint, streamlined, precise forms, simplicity and regularity; what he wanted, but constantly distanced himself from by beating the wings of his great visionary talent, was attempted with more energetic consistency by Cubism.

Cubism in architecture — and this must be clearly understood — arose completely independently, absolutely free of Wright, in a manner analogous to and driven by painting and sculpture, from an inner urge.

Apart from superficial, outward resemblances, there was probably also a distant inner kinship with Wright's works — this would merit further study and in this respect some of Wright's reliefs should also be examined — although both are absolutely different in their nature, and indeed opposites.

They appear to agree in an urge to incorporate the rectangular, in a tendency towards the three-dimensional, in the way in which the massing of the buildings is broken down and reassembled, and generally in efforts to combine many small elements — initially obtained by disassembling — into a whole whose appearance still betrays the elements of the original analysis; further elements they have in common: the use of new materials, new techniques, new constructions, the concentration of new demands.

However, what was exuberant sculpture, sensory excess in Wright's oeuvre became puritanical asceticism, spiritual abstinence in Cubism — that could initially not be any other way. What unfolded in Wright's work out of the abundance of life, moving towards an opulence that could only suit American "high life," reined itself back in again in Europe, into an abstraction that was rooted in other ideals and encompassed everything and everyone.

While Wright proved in practice to be more of an artist than a prophet, Cubism prepared more aggressively to realize what was also his theory.

The conscience of architecture — after being shaken awake for thirty years — has spoken again for the first time since the Renaissance; with painstaking precision, as is typical of puberty, but also just as forcefully.

As in the liberal "arts," architecture was in a transitional stage: a stage of breaking away from the old system and constructing a new order. The concept of the structural system and the value of proportions were regained and elevated to a higher level; the essential meaning of the line and the almost oppressive seriousness of form were acknowledged anew and explored down to the last detail; insight into the importance of massing and its complement: space, was recovered and examined in depth again. Above all, however, Cubism — as a logical continuation of earlier attempts at renewal — directly and forcefully expressed the tension of a greater and more genuine vitality than found in the architecture of many previous epochs, in which independent living was until recently at most limited to the sweet and touching dexterity of well-cultivated taste endowed with a virtuoso talent for composition.

Cubism was thus a form of reflection and a beginning; it imposed obligations, trusting in the future, whereas previous generations had borrowed rights, parasitizing the past. In the unintentional romanticism of its convulsive urge to draw everything together, it constituted an attempt to create a new synthesis of forms, a new — ahistorical — classicism.

The precursors to the need for numbers and proportion, for purity and order, for regularity and repetition, for perfection and completeness; characteristics of the organs of modern life, technology, transport, hygiene, inherent also in the nature of society, economic conditions, methods of mass production, can all be found in Cubism.

The tragedy is that the development of matters that Wright advocated for so long and so vigorously has been damaged by incomprehension of his work, as well as suffering from the superficial posturing of his own disciples. We can remain indifferent to the way in which the conception of the master builder expanded beyond the preacher's consciousness: indifferent because of the beautiful result, indifferent because the basis of his work is upright and not tarnished in advance by aesthetic premises, indifferent ultimately because life that has not degenerated into paralysis continually eludes the dogma of theory — and a good thing too!

Nevertheless, theory — as should be emphasized — is highly valuable as a foundation in life. It is always valuable, but is completely indispensable in these times that lack every aesthetic yardstick, every traditional stronghold. The new architecture cannot be consistent enough in its pursuit of its goals: we will gladly — if they deserve it! — take on board the inevitable inconsistencies of its results.

It cannot be repeated too often to Wright's disciples — as he did himself — that building on Wright's oeuvre is somewhat different from what is commonly dubbed "drawing inspiration" from his work.

It is no less problematic to imitate something built by a contemporary than it is to imitate a Greek column: on the contrary. The obstacles that academic architecture puts in the way of the emergence of a functional architecture are even more harmful, as are the products of the imitators of modern predecessors, because the second-hand extrinsic elements in which these imitators robe their work, through its contemporary form and the gesture of organic becoming, avoids the controversy concerning pure building precisely where advocates of academic architecture openly offer a flank to attack. And if anything is "detrimental" to the future of a new architecture, it is this half-measure, which is annoying as public plagiarism, as a lack of character.

1925

INDEX OF ILLUSTRATIONS

IM **ALBERT LANGEN VERLAG MÜNCHEN**

ERSCHEINEN DIE

BAUHAUSBÜCHER

Schriftleitung: WALTER GROPIUS und L. MOHOLY-NAGY

Die ersten 10 Bände sind erschienen:

1	**Walter Gropius**	INTERNATIONALE ARCHITEKTUR.
2	**Paul Klee**	PÄDAGOGISCHES SKIZZENBUCH.
3	**Ein Versuchshaus des Bauhauses**	
4	**Die Bühne im Bauhaus**	
5	**Piet Mondrian**	NEUE GESTALTUNG.
6	**Theo van Doesburg**	GRUNDBEGRIFFE DER NEUEN GESTALTENDEN KUNST.
7	**Neue Arbeiten der Bauhauswerkstätten**	
8	**L. Moholy-Nagy**	MALEREI, PHOTOGRAPHIE, FILM.
9	**W. Kandinsky**	PUNKT UND LINIE ZU FLÄCHE.
10	**J. J. P. Oud**	HOLLÄNDISCHE ARCHITEKTUR.

IN VORBEREITUNG:

KURT SCHWITTERS: MERZ-BUCH
HEINRICH JACOBY: SCHÖPFERISCHE MUSIKERZIEHUNG
GEORGE ANTHEIL (AMERIKA): MUSICO-MECHANICO
ALBERT GLEIZES (FRANKREICH): KUBISMUS
F. T. MARINETTI UND E. PRAMPOLINI (ITALIEN): FUTURISMUS
FRITZ WICHERT: EXPRESSIONISMUS
TRISTAN TZARA UND HANS ARP: DADAISMUS
L. KASSAK UND E. KALLAI (UNGARN): DIE MA-GRUPPE
T. van DOESBURG (HOLLAND): DIE STIJLGRUPPE
CAREL TEIGE (PRAG): TSCHECHISCHE KUNST
LOUIS LOZKWICK (AMERIKA): AMERIKANISCHE ARCHITEKTUR
WALTER GROPIUS: NEUE ARCHITEKTURDARSTELLUNG
DAS FLACHE DACH. MONTIERBARE TYPENBAUTEN.
DIE BAUHAUSNEUBAUTEN IN DESSAU
MIES VAN DER ROHE: ÜBER ARCHITEKTUR
LE CORBUSIER (FRANKREICH): ÜBER ARCHITEKTUR
K. LÖNBERG-HOLM (DÄNEMARK): ÜBER ARCHITEKTUR
FRIEDRICH KIESLER (ÖSTERREICH): NEUE FORMEN DER DEMONSTRATION. DIE RAUMSTADT
JANE HEAP (AMERIKA): DIE NEUE WELT
G. MUCHE UND R. PAULICK: DAS METALLTYPENHAUS
MART STAM: DAS „ABC" VOM BAUEN
RAOUL HAUSMANN: OPTOPHONETIK
MAX BURCHARTZ: GESTALTUNG
MARTIN SCHÄFER: KONSTRUKTIVE BIOLOGIE
REKLAME UND TYPOGRAPHIE DES BAUHAUSES
L. MOHOLY-NAGY: AUFBAU DER GESTALTUNGEN
PAUL KLEE: BILDNERISCHE MECHANIK
OSKAR SCHLEMMER: BÜHNENELEMENTE
JOOST SCHMIDT: BILDERMAGAZIN DER ZEIT
DIE NEUEN KÜNSTLICHEN MATERIALIEN
J. ALBERS: FUNKTIONSFORMEN
ADOLF BEHNE: KUNST, HANDWERK UND INDUSTRIE
W. KANDINSKY: VIOLETT (BÜHNENSTÜCK)

At LARS MÜLLER PUBLISHERS the following titles are available in English translation and original design

Bauhausbücher

1 International Architecture by Walter Gropius
ISBN 978-3-03778-584-3
2 Pedagogical Sketchbook by Paul Klee
ISBN 978-3-03778-585-0
3 A Bauhaus Experimental House by Adolf Meyer
ISBN 978-3-03778-627-7
4 The Theater of the Bauhaus by Oskar Schlemmer
ISBN 978-3-03778-628-4
5 New Design by Piet Mondrian
ISBN 978-3-03778-586-7
6 Principles of Neo-Plastic Art by Theodor van Doesburg
ISBN 978-3-03778-629-1
7 New Works from the Bauhaus Workshops by Walter Gropius
ISBN 978-3-03778-630-7
8 Painting, Photography, Film by László Moholy-Nagy
ISBN 978-3-03778-587-4
9 Point and Line to Plane by Wassily Kandinsky
ISBN 978-3-03778-662-8
10 Dutch Architecture by Jacobus Johannes Pieter Oud
ISBN 978-3-03778-663-5
11 The Non-objective World by Kasimir Malevich
ISBN 978-3-03778-664-2
12 Bauhaus Buildings Dessau by Walter Gropius
ISBN 978-3-03778-665-9
13 Cubism by Albert Gleizes
ISBN 978-3-03778-666-6
14 From Material to Architecture by László Moholy-Nagy
ISBN 978-3-03778-667-3

bauhaus journal 1926–1931
Facsimile edition with commentary
ISBN 978-3-03778-588-1, English
ISBN 978-3-03778-594-2, German

State Bauhaus in Weimar 1919–1923
Facsimile edition with commentary
ISBN 978-3-03778-623-9, English
ISBN 978-3-03778-620-8, German

www.lars-mueller-publishers.com

Jacobus Johannes Pieter Oud
Dutch Architecture
Bauhausbücher 10 (1926)

It will soon be 100 years since Walter Gropius and László Moholy-Nagy made the grand gesture of initiating and publishing the *Bauhausbücher* series. Their intention to document and disseminate in book form the New Design philosophy in all areas of its application testifies to the enthusiasm that prevailed at the Bauhaus. However, only a quarter of the planned titles had been published by 1930. Political turmoil and war thwarted the further expansion of the series. The original editions are almost impossible to find today.

The goal of my initiative is to gradually make the fourteen *Bauhausbücher* available again in a form true to the originals and–in some cases for the first time–in English translation. With this project I am fulfilling my own bibliophile passion and my conviction that there is no future without a past. Only a solid knowledge of history can open up perspectives on how we can take advantage of the insights gleaned by modernism while also transcending them.

Lars Müller

The *Bauhausbücher* in this edition are designed to resemble as closely as possible the German originals from the 1920s. The typographical layout and distinguishing elements were imitated, and the look of the lead typefaces used at the time was simulated as closely as possible using today's digital technology. A concession had to be made in the choice of paper, however. The pulp used one hundred years ago with its high wood content naturally led to a yellowish paper. We assume that at the time the designers chose the whitest paper available and have therefore selected a white paper in common use today for reprinting the *Bauhausbücher.* For the cover, embossing and jacket design of our series, we have opted for a unified interpretation of the historical German book originals.

With the aim of raising the profile of the Bauhaus at home and abroad, in 1923 Walter Gropius and his newly appointed colleague László Moholy-Nagy–an artist already well versed in both the design and the targeted use of media–conceived the idea of a series of books. Over the next three years, they planned altogether fifty-four titles by different authors on a wide variety of subjects, in slim volumes that could be quickly produced. Ranging from natural sciences, literature, politics and religion to almost all the "isms" of art, the series encompassed a spectrum testifying to little short of a utopian vision (one of the proposed volumes was indeed titled *Utopisches*): to forge a connection, in terms of content, between the entire phenomena of the modern world and the avant-garde school, and to harness this knowledge for the future design of every sphere of daily life. Due to financial problems, the first eight books in this ambitious program only appeared in 1925, published by the Albert Langen Verlag. A further four volumes followed in the years up to 1928, while Gropius and Moholy-Nagy were still at the Bauhaus, and even after their departure two more also appeared under their editorship up to 1930. The two subsequent directors of the school, Hannes Meyer and Ludwig Mies van der Rohe, did not continue the *Bauhausbücher*. According to the original publicity leaflet of 1925, the fourteen published volumes in the series examine "artistic, scientific and technical issues ... from the point of view of their mutual relation." Six of the teachers at the Bauhaus–Walter Gropius, László Moholy-Nagy, Paul Klee, Adolf Meyer, Oskar Schlemmer and Wassily Kandinsky–authored nine books on their respective theoretical and educational approaches and on Bauhaus products; the remaining volumes focused on trends in art closely akin to the Bauhaus. Available in both paperback and a linen binding, the editions of around 3,000 copies usually sold out quickly and were often printed a second time. Despite the different design of their covers, the volumes are recognizable as a series thanks to their uniform format, abundance of illustrations, and their distinctive design and layout by Moholy-Nagy, characterized by striking contrasts of blank space and sans serif font, as well as by letters and graphic elements deployed for visual effect. With their compelling interplay of content and form, the *Bauhausbücher* are still today considered milestones of avant-garde book production.

Astrid Bähr
Bauhaus-Archiv / Museum für Gestaltung, Berlin

About *Dutch Architecture*

1926 saw the publication of Jacobus Johannes Pieter Oud's *Dutch Architecture,* a further volume from Dutch De Stijl circles in the wake of Piet Mondrian's *New Design* and Theo van Doesburg's *Principles of Neo-Plastic Art.* Editors Walter Gropius and László Moholy-Nagy thus not only accorded this movement the most prominent position in the *Bauhausbücher* series alongside their own views but also kept their promise to disseminate in-depth insights into European artistic creation. Like several of the preceding volumes, this publication developed out of the first major Bauhaus exhibition, held in Weimar in 1923. Walter Gropius had presumably become aware of the Dutch architect, writer, and cofounder of the De Stijl artists group through their mutual acquaintance, Adolf Behne, who had written about Oud in *Wasmuths Monatshefte* in 1921. In particular, Oud's municipal housing projects attracted great attention among architects of the *Neues Bauen* [New Building] movement in Germany, as it was hoped that this would provide momentum and an important stimulus to realize urgently necessary schemes of this type. Furthermore in the same year, Gropius and Oud also encountered each other as direct rivals in the competition to design the Kallenbach House in Berlin-Grunewald, in which the Dutchman's proposal, characterized by clearly defined volumes, prevailed over the Expressionist blueprint drawn up by Gropius and Adolf Meyer's studio. Another connection may have come about through Theo van Doesburg, De Stijl's most important advocate, who was in Weimar in 1921/22 and decisively influenced the Bauhaus during this period. Be that as it may, Gropius asked Oud to propose Dutch architects whose works he wanted to include in a presentation of international architecture as part of the Bauhaus exhibition. In addition, he convinced Oud to appear as a guest speaker at the Bauhaus Week held at the start of the exhibition in August 1923–a particular honor, as, apart from Gropius, who talked about the new path pursued by the school under the slogan "Art and Technology–A New Unity," the only other speaker was Wassily Kandinsky.

"The Development of Modern Architecture in The Netherlands," a 70-page lecture with 39 architectural photographs and designs that Oud had previously presented in Berlin and Magdeburg and also gave in other European cities in subsequent years is simultaneously the centerpiece of *Dutch Architecture*. In it, Oud sketches out a developmental lineage, taking works by his teacher Pierre Cuypers as his point of departure, with a view to deriving general guidelines for a new architecture. This lineage begins with Hendrik Berlage's buildings, the first to be adapted to the needs of modern life and technology, runs through the representatives of the Amsterdam School, whom he still regards as being overly attached to romantic

Jacobus Johannes Pieter Oud * February 9, 1890, in Purmerend, Netherlands; † April 5, 1963, in Wassenaar, Netherlands. Oud was educated in Amsterdam and at the Delft Technical University, after which he worked in the offices of the architects Petrus Josephus Hubertus Cuypers, Jan Stuyt and Theodor Fischer. In 1917 he was one of the cofounders of the De Stijl movement, along with Theo van Doesburg and Piet Mondrian. From 1918 onward, through Hendrik Petrus Berlage's mediation, Oud worked as an architect for the city of Rotterdam. The housing blocks he designed and built at Spangen (1918), Tusschendijken (1920) and Hoek van Holland (1924–27) had a sober and functional austerity. In 1920 he founded the group Opbouw. One year later he met Walter Gropius and László Moholy-Nagy in Weimar. Shortly afterwards, he broke with van Doesburg and De Stijl. In 1923 Oud participated in the Bauhaus Week and the International Architecture Exhibition.

According to advertisements printed in the back of some volumes of the *Bauhausbücher* as well as in pre-order brochures elsewhere, the following further titles were planned to be published in the series, but never realized due to the events of the time:

Josef Albers, *Funktionsformen* (Functional Forms)
George Antheil, *Musico-Mechanico* (Musico-Mechanico)
Hans Arp and Tristan Tzara, *Dadaismus* (Dadaism)
Adolf Behne, *Kunst, Handwerk und Industrie* (Art, Craft and Industry)
Adolf Behne, *Russland* (Russia)
Adolf Behne and Max Burchartz / Max Burchartz, *Plastik der Gestaltungen* (Sculpture of Designs)
Max Burchartz, *Gestaltung* (Design)
Walter Gropius, *Neue Architekturdarstellung* (New Architecture Representation)
Walter Gropius, *Das flache Dach. Montierbare Typenbauten* (The Flat Roof. Mountable Type Buildings)
Raoul Hausmann, *Optophonetik* (Optophonetics)
Jane Heap, *Die neue Welt* (The New World)
Heinrich Jacoby, *Schöpferische Musikerziehung* (Creative Musical Education)
Ernő Kállai and Lajos Kassák, *Die Arbeit der MA-Gruppe / Die MA-Gruppe* (The Work of the MA Group / The MA Group)
Wassily Kandinsky, *Violett (Bühnenstück mit Einleitung und Szenerie)* (Violet [Stage Play with Introduction and Scenery])
Friedrich Kiesler, *Neue Formen der Demonstration. Die Raumstadt* (New Forms of Demonstration. The Space City)
Paul Klee, *Bildnerische Mechanik* (Pictorial Mechanics)
Le Corbusier / Le Corbusier-Saugnier [Saugnier: Amédée Ozenfant], *Über Architektur* (On Architecture)
El Lissitzky, *Reklame und Typographie* (Advertisement and Typography)
Knud Lonberg-Holm, *Über Architektur* (On Architecture)
Louis Lozowick, *Amerikanische Architektur* (American Architecture)
Filippo Tommaso Marinetti and Enrico Prampolini, *Futurismus* (Futurism)
Adolf Meyer, *Die neuen Materialen* (The New Materials)
Ludwig Mies van der Rohe, *Über Architektur* (On Architecture)
László Moholy-Nagy, *Werkarbeit der Gestaltungen* (Workmanship of Designs)
László Moholy-Nagy, *Aufbau der Gestaltungen* (Structure of Designs)
Georg Muche, *Amerika?–Europa* (America?–Europe)
Georg Muche and Richard Paulick, *Das Metall Typenhaus* (The Metal Type House)
Martin Schäfer, *Konstruktive Biologie* (Constructive Biology)
Oskar Schlemmer, *Bildermagazin der Zeit I* (Image Journal of the Time I)
Oskar Schlemmer, *Bühnenelemente* (Elements of Theater)
Joost Schmidt, *Bildermagazin der Zeit II* (Image Journal of the Time II)
Kurt Schwitters, *Merz-Buch* (Merz Book)
Mart Stam, *Das "ABC" vom Bauen* (The "ABC" of Building)
Karel Teige, *Tschechische Kunst* (Czech Art)
Theo van Doesburg, *Die Arbeit der Stijl-Gruppe / Die Stijl-Gruppe* (The Work of the De Stijl Group / The Stijl Group)
Fritz Wichert, *Expressionismus* (Expressionism)

N.N., *Architektur, Malerei, Plastik aus den Werkstätten des Bauhauses* (Architecture, Painting, Sculpture from the Bauhaus Workshops)
N.N., *Die neuen künstlichen Materialien* (The New Artificial Materials)
N.N., *Kleinwohnungen von der Architekturabteilung des* Bauhauses (Small Apartments from the Architecture Department of the Bauhaus)
N.N., *Reklame und Typographie des Bauhauses* (Advertisement and Typography of the Bauhaus)

Varying authors and titles are indicated with a slash.

At Lars Müller Publishers, the complete 14-volume series of the *Bauhausbücher* is available:

1 Walter Gropius, *International Architecture,* 1925 (2019),
ISBN 978-3-03778-584-3
2 Paul Klee, *Pedagogical Sketchbook,* 1925 (2019),
ISBN 978-3-03778-585-0
3 Adolf Meyer, *A Bauhaus Experimental House,* 1925 (2020),
ISBN 978-3-03778-627-7
4 Oskar Schlemmer, *The Theater of the Bauhaus,* 1925 (2020),
ISBN 978-3-03778-628-4
5 Piet Mondrian, *New Design,* 1925 (2019),
ISBN 978-3-03778-586-7
6 Theo van Doesburg, *Principles of Neo-Plastic Art,* 1925 (2020),
ISBN 978-3-03778-629-1
7 Walter Gropius, *New Works from the Bauhaus Workshops,* 1925 (2020),
ISBN 978-3-03778-630-7
8 László Moholy-Nagy, *Painting, Photography, Film,* 1925 (2019),
ISBN 978-3-03778-587-4
9 Wassily Kandinsky, *Point and Line to Plane,* 1926 (2021),
ISBN 978-3-03778-662-8
10 Jacobus Johannes Pieter Oud, *Dutch Architecture,* 1926 (2021),
ISBN 978-3-03778-663-5
11 Kasimir Malevich, *The Non-objective World,* 1927 (2021),
ISBN 978-3-03778-664-2
12 Walter Gropius, *Bauhaus Buildings Dessau,* 1930 (2021),
ISBN 978-3-03778-665-9
13 Albert Gleizes, *Cubism,* 1928 (2021),
ISBN 978-3-03778-666-6
14 László Moholy-Nagy, *From Material to Architecture,* 1929 (2021),
ISBN 978-3-03778-667-3

bauhaus journal 1926–1931
Facsimile edition with commentary (2019)
ISBN 978-3-03778-588-1, English
ISBN 978-3-03778-594-2, German

State Bauhaus in Weimar 1919–1923
Facsimile edition with commentary (2019)
ISBN 978-3-03778-623-9, English
ISBN 978-3-03778-620-8, German

www.lars-mueller-publishers.com/bauhaus

Image credits:
Cover images 3 and 4, 20, 21, 25–29, 31–34, 36: © 2021, ProLitteris, Zurich
37: © F.L.C. / 2021, ProLitteris, Zurich
38: © Bauhaus-Archiv Berlin / VG Bild-Kunst
We have endeavored to identify all copyright holders. Should despite our intensive research any person entitled to rights have been overlooked, they are kindly requested to contact the publisher.

Jacobus Johannes Pieter Oud
Dutch Architecture
Bauhausbücher 10 (1926)
First English Edition (2021)

Editor: Lars Müller
Foreword and commentary: Astrid Bähr
Project management: Miriam Eickhoff
Translation: Helen Ferguson
Translation (leaflet): Jennifer Taylor, Karen Williams, Helen Ferguson
Proofreading: Keonaona Peterson
Typesetting and production: Esther Butterworth
Lithography, printing and binding: DZA Druckerei zu Altenburg, Germany
Paper: Infinity Silk, 135 gsm
Typefaces: LD Genzsch Antiqua, Akzidenz-Grotesk Pro

The German original *Holländische Architektur* was published in 1926 by Albert Langen Verlag München.

Lars Müller Publishers is supported by the Swiss Federal Office of Culture with a structural contribution for the years 2021–2024.

Lars Müller Publishers
Zurich, Switzerland
www.lars-mueller-publishers.com

ISBN 978-3-03778-663-5

Distributed in North America by ARTBOOK | D.A.P.
www.artbook.com

Printed in Germany

We thank the Bauhaus-Archiv / Museum für Gestaltung, Berlin, for their advice and support.

Published with the generous support of the Rudolf-August Oetker-Stiftung.